Caravaggio

romaeditrice

An unlearned genius

Caravaggio is certainly a borderline case in the Italian and European history of art. Even if he was the most gifted realists in the history of painting, his art mirrors the platonic philosophic concept according to which the truth of things is conceived as the conscience of the world. For Caravaggio everything was worth becoming a work of art. What was inconvenient for his clients, had enough dignity for him to be represented. He was deeply interested in setting apart from the Catholic concept of artistic representation to which he opposed his art made of flesh and blood, free from the false decorum of Mannerism.

He had not pupils, as he had not a workshop where to educate them on the art of painting; he left a crowded host of emulators and plagiarists, but also a group of great artists, such as Orazio Gentileschi, Battistello Caracciolo, Guercino in the '10s, Bartolomeo Manfredi. However his name is numbered among the exceptions to rediscover. Not even the century of realism – 1800 – was able to find the right conditions to correctly evaluate the Lombard genius. That was caused by a certain nationalism, which in Italy preferred to draw from the

BIOGRAPHY

He is officially said to be born in Caravaggio, a village between Milan and Bergamo, in 1571. But more probably his birthplace was Milan.

His father was Fermo Merisi, "magister" of the house of Marquis Francesco I Sforza; his mother was Lucia Aratori. He had a complete Lombard painting education.

endless and rather bulky heritage of Renaissance. However we should keep in mind that the contemporary vision of art, which bases its principles on the binomial art-life – as a criterion to evaluate a talent - did not exist in the 17th century. Caravaggio was able to fuse each expression of nature in the beauty of art. And he did it because of his scornful passion of man, following his own instinct and not a school of thought. He drew his models from life – either baskets full of fruit or exuberant and ambiguous young men in inns, or even he himself with a certain realism far from staging and pretence. For this reason, the shining spark of his fame lasted only until the 1630s. The century of the Baroque did not appreciate this

brutal and scornful vision of the tangible world. Caravaggio exceeded that vision, went beyond it, fixed life and death in concrete things and he revealed as those two elements were at the same time alive in the experience of the tangible body. In a basket of ▶

fruit you can see luxuriant leaves and withered leaves. Each body is dominated by those two opposite and complementary principles. We see the same in the dreamy, dull and quite ironic expression in the frown of "Bacchus": it smells of life, but in a disturbing way it is the mortal cause of his ineluctable caducity, expressed in the sick complexion and in the weakly whitish lips.

This Caravaggesque vision of the human being derives from a tragic awareness, from the historic solitude which the sensitive universe of nature and bodies is doomed to. "An unlearned man, but a genius" as incisively defined him Alois Riegl, one of the greatest representatives of the School of Wien. A "genius" overwhelmed by the science of truth, condemned to die during his most shining flash of life. However, an "unlearned man" can be endowed with a free acumen. Caravaggio's intellectual freedom was unbridled; certain philosophical, moral and theoretic intuitions became real just for his very refined common sense which leads his eye and hand. ∎

5

He was an apprentice of Simone Peterzano, a late Mannerist devoted to formal Mannerism, widespread in his times. With Peterzano, Caravaggio came in contact with the Lombard tradition which began to spread in the first half of the 16th century by the artists Savoldo and Moretto. He was much influenced by Tiziano's painting, whose "Crowning with Thorns" he probably studied (today in the Louvre).

Sick
Bacchus

The work is listed among the paintings confiscated to Cavalier d'Arpino by the revenue in 1607 and donated by Pope Paul V to his nephew Cardinal Scipione Borghese. It is among Caravaggio's earliest paintings (around 1591).

Some critics, according to Bellori, consider it a self-portrait, made in the period during which the artist was in hospital from malaria (the title itself of the painting, suggested by Longhi for the livid face characterizing the figure, is a clear example of it). Other critics, more than considering it a portrayal of the god of wine, state it is just the portrait of the person who posed as a model.

The detailed naturalistic analysis of the subject, made by Caravaggio, shows only a young man crowned with vine leaves, with a bunch of grapes in his hand – an image so far from the magniloquent exteriority of the god of wine, in the iconography. The fruit and the vine are a sort of extraordinary prelude to Caravaggio's "Boy with a Basket of Fruit". Since the first moment, Caravaggio's naturalism is revolutionary and shocking. ■

BIOGRAPHY

In 1590 Caravaggio's mother died (his father, Fermo died in 1577, when the young Michelangelo was six years old). According to his most ancient biographers (Giuliano Mancini, Giovanni Baglione, Giovan Pietro Bellori), two years later, at twenty, he settled in Rome. The difficulties he had at the beginning of his stay were clearly linked to his sustenance and the unease due to his temperament, which did not fit in with the vaguely scornful intellectual atmosphere of the Eternal City.

The Fortune
Teller

1594 – Rome,
Musei Capitolini

The genre scene represents a gypsy woman who, while reading a young man's hand, skilfully stole him a ring from his finger. Referring to the planning of the work, Bellori (1672) narrates a vivid anecdote "(…) he called the girl who was passing by and, taken her to the hotel, he portrayed her in the act of foretelling the future, as those Egyptian women usually do".

The model used by Caravaggio is not historic, neither mythological nor religious. Caravaggio prefers a naturalistic and moral aspect that sounds revolutionary in the late Mannerism, which still refused such artistic expressions.

The cunning deceit is extraordinarily expressed by the two characters and by the scene in which "the young gypsy shows her astuteness, smiling feigningly in stealing the ring" (G. Mancini, 1617-21). The harsh representation of the gypsy's dirty nails belongs to modern naturalism – the dramatic reality which is stronger in Caravaggio than the oration in praise or the myth. ■

BIOGRAPHY

He started out in the workshops of Lorenzo Siciliano and Antiveduto Grammatica, and then he was "employed" by Giuseppe Cesari, known as Cavalier d'Arpino – a famous late Mannerist painter who delegated the young Caravaggio, already skilful in naturalistic investigations, "to paint flowers and fruit". In Cavalier d'Arpino's workshop, Merisi specialized in painting still life – a genre in which the Lombard artist soon showed his innovative character.

Boy
with a basket of fruit

T he subject of the boy with a basket of fruit derives from a theme dear to Lombard Naturalism. Thus the young Caravaggio looks for the same optic and natural "truth", the same researched by his predecessors in painting.

For Caravaggio, still life was as important as figure painting. So the representation of fruit – detailed to be precisely identified – is radical and has an allegorical and symbolic meaning, typical of the complex personality of the artist. The painting, made early in the Roman period, emerges to fill the natural gap between the subject and the eye of the person who looks at it, through a direct view reproduction, which reminds us of Giorgione's Venetian portraits. ■

BIOGRAPHY

The activities of the first Roman years centred above all on genre scenes paintings with such a harsh directness, now far from the need to historicize the cultural atmosphere around him. In those years Caravaggio was already isolated. He was rushed to hospital for a malaria attack, as witnessed in the famous self-portrait "Sick Bacchus" in the Borghese Gallery.

Adolescent
Bacchus

1593/94
Florence, Uffizi

"The first was Bacchus with some bunches of different grapes, made with great care". The biographer Baglione clearly shows that the "new fact" of Caravaggio's painting – that is the representation of true nature at the expense of idealization – appeared to be soon clear to his contemporaries. The naturalistic themes introduced in this work by Merisi are authentic pictorial virtuosities: note the details of the rippling surface of wine and the reflexes of the subject on the jug. The symbolic value of each element of still life is an allegory of seasonal cycles (fruit), alluding – through the representation of the dead and resurrected Greek God Dionysus – to the mystery of redemption. ∎

BIOGRAPHY

He spent brawling years of a squalid life and straitened circumstances, until in 1595 he met Cardinal Francesco Del Monte, who gave him his favour, elevated him to the status of prominent artist in the Roman circles.

Since then Caravaggio's painting, after the narrow borders of his anonymity, became a means of sensational innovative power which shattered men of learning, artists and prelates.

The lute
player

1594 – Saint Petersburg,
Hermitage

One of the main features of Caravaggio's early paintings is the exaltation of the ephebic beauty, here accompanied by music.

The work was considered a crystalline masterpiece by the critics. It was painted for Cardinal Del Monte, in whose palace musical entertainments were performed by the most important musicians of Rome during the papacy of Clement VIII. The young man represented in the painting, with the open shirt and a dreamy gaze, is caught in still lives of astonishing pictorial accuracy: a violin, some musical scores, fruit, vegetables and flowers.

The picture is a sort of allegory to music and love, according to a theme recurrent in the 16th century painting. ■

BIOGRAPHY

His commissions increased at the same rate as the scandals where the artist was protagonist. Countless fights, wounds, duels, brawls filled his life. The 17th c. Spanish way of life - that of the "bravi"- emphasized his untameable temperament.

Rest on flight
to Egypt

*1594/96 – Rome,
Doria Pamphili Gallery*

An atmosphere of serene sweetness characterizes this early painting by Caravaggio – his first biblical subject of big size. The work represents a rest of the sacred family visited by an angel musician, with his back to the viewer, while reading a score held by St Joseph. Note that the notes on the score are not random, but they follow a model written by the Flemish composer Noel Bauldwijn. That is a motet, taken from the Songs of Songs in honour to the Virgin which starts with the words "Quam pulchra es" ("How fair art thou"). The light peacefully spreading on the scene is quite far from the harsh light cuts, typical of the Lombard artist. The naturalistic landscape and the green details in the foreground of astonishing accuracy, recall the Leonardesque figure of the artist-scientist. ■

BIOGRAPHY

That was a sort of emotional violent exasperation, tangible also in his works, which brought Caravaggio to the fatal, probably unintentional killing of Ranuccio Tomassoni from Terni. A furious brawl burst over a disputed score in the racket game, in the court of Muro Torto (below Villa Medici), during which Tomassoni won ten escudos from Caravaggio.

Judith
and Holofernes

// (Judith) went to the bed, took his head by his hair and said: "Strengthen me, O Lord God of Israel, in this hour". And, with all her strength, she struck twice upon his neck, and cut off his head" (Judith 13, 7-9).

The harsh biblical subject, the hard sharpness of the death represented which is the beginning of a long series of paintings in which the artist analyzes the tragic meaning of life, did not let this work be appreciated soon by the critics-even the 20th century's. The pictorial behaviour is typical of Caravaggio's early maturity. Caravaggio is soon identified in the expressive energy of the faces and in the naturalistic details, in the immediate action and in the study of the contrasting effects of light. We can note a Lombard origin - even Leonardesque, as in the Medusa in the Uffizi, in the movements of the faces and in the physiological reflexes of the characters.

After Caravaggio's interpretation of this subject there followed a huge and lucky series of works, on the same theme, by some of the most relevant Caravaggesque painters: Valentin de Boulogne and Adam Elsheimer. ■

BIOGRAPHY

The homicide obliged him to flee Rome in terror of the juridical consequences of his act. It was May 1606 – this date marks the beginning of the Caravaggesque "Odyssey".
At first the artist sought refuge in the estate of Prince Marzio Colonna, situated nearby Palestrina, Paliano and Zagarolo. Eventually he reached Naples, under the sovereignty of another government, while his protectors in Rome worked to have an amnesty.

Basket
of fruit

For a long time this work has been considered, by mistake, the first still life in the history of Italian art. Anyway the "Basket of Fruit" is the founder of modern painting and it witnesses Caravaggio's intellectual stature.

Beyond the immediate technical skill in representing reality, the detail which makes this still life special is its dramatic dimension.

The realism of its description goes up to the details of the wormy apples and to the withering leaves.

That is an existential meditation, a recall to the presence of death and caducity beside life. ■

BIOGRAPHY

He spent nearly a year in Naples, leaving a remarkable sign in the early 17th century cultural life of a wealthy city crowded with aristocrats, middle class men and courtiers. Then he travelled to the island of Malta, wishing to get the cross of the Knight of the Order; he arrived there towards the end of 1607. In July 1608 he was received as a Knight of Grace into the Order of Malta for his artistic merits.

Medusa

Painted on a canvas mounted on a wooden tournament shield, the "Medusa" was commissioned by Cardinal Del Monte and donated to the Grand Duke of Tuscany, Ferdinando.

The poet Giovan Battista Marino wrote about this work: "Quel fiero Gorgone, e crudo / cui fanno horribilmente / volumi viperini / squallida pompa, e spaventosa à i crini".

The representation of Gorgon – a common iconographic motif among the artists of all times – is a sort of horrid wonder, even more emphasized by the gruesome details of the snakes and the furious jet of blood.

All Caravaggio's typical expressionistic inclinations are seen in Medusa's terrible scream, in her wide-open eyes and facial spasm. ■

22

BIOGRAPHY

In October 1608, a criminal commission summoned by a procurator, who knew the real reasons of the artist's flight from Rome, compelled Caravaggio to flee again.

Landed in Sicily, at Syracuse, which he left in the first months of 1609 to reach Messina and then Palermo.

The Calling
of St Matthew

The three works made by Caravaggio for the Contarelli Chapel in San Luigi dei Francesi are the first important commission given in Rome to the artist. As the biographer Baglione said, Cardinal Del Monte's good words (Caravaggio's protector) were behind the commission. The iconographic program had been fixed many years before, in 1565, by Contarelli himself. According to the X-rays, the planning of the three works was hard and delayed for the continuous second thoughts of the artist. The painting represents the episode narrated in the Acts. Seated at a table and counting some money, the tax gatherer Levi d'Alfeo – St Matthew's name before he became the apostle – was summoned by Christ to spread God's words. The imperious gesture of Christ, accompanied by a low and highly symbolic light, is the theme which dominates and determines the picture. Seven are the characters represented: their movements and the expressive strength in their faces favour and accompany the visual development of the narration, from right to left, converging in the figure of Matthew. ■

BIOGRAPHY

During the Sicilian stay, Caravaggio was shattered, anxious and prostrate. Awaiting the papal pardon made him restless, almost insane. The island seemed to him an inadequate place for his desperate greatness. Rome kept on coming back into his mind, forcefully.

Martyrdom
of St Matthew

*1599/1600 – Rome,
San Luigi dei Francesi*

The final reorganization of this work was the result of long meditations. In effect, the X-rays brought to light a previous setting among ancient architectures, inspired to late Raffaello, but soon given up for a full vision of the bodies inspired by Michelangelo.

The centre of the action is the Ethiopian soldier, sent by king Hirtacus to prevent the saint from his religious proselytism. Matthew is on the ground, while the other horrified characters watching the scene seem to detach from it, as swept away by a centrifugal stream: only the angel seems to be out of this strength – he appears as a cloud giving the palm of martyrdom to Matthew.

Today it is astonishing to think that such a painting was done without a drawing. ■

BIOGRAPHY

During his march to Rome, he stopped in Naples. In the meantime, the intervention of Cardinal Gonzaga gave him another chance to have the papal pardon. But bad luck pursued him once more: the painter was attacked and wounded so badly by Maltese emissaries at the door of the German inn of the Cerriglio where he lodged. His conditions appeared so desperate that rumours said that the painter was dead.

St Matthew
and the Angel

The painting in the Contarelli Chapel is the second version of the picture made by Caravaggio. The first version for the altar – representing the saint as a folk man – (destroyed in Berlin in 1945) was rejected by the Contarelli heirs, perhaps for the excessive realism in the interpretation of the subject. The composition has a sinusoidal progress, starting from the top figure of the angel inspiring St Matthew.

Particularly charming is the detail of the counting hands. Note the stool with the knee of the saint on, such extemporarily instable to stress Matthew's moment of wonder for the arrival of the angel, helped by the almost bare setting of the action. ∎

BIOGRAPHY

During his long convalescence he painted other masterpieces, such as "Salome with the Head of the Baptist" and the tragic "David with the Head of Goliath", in which he painfully portrayed himself in the face of the beheaded giant. In the mid of July 1610 he sailed on board a felucca to the Latium coasts.

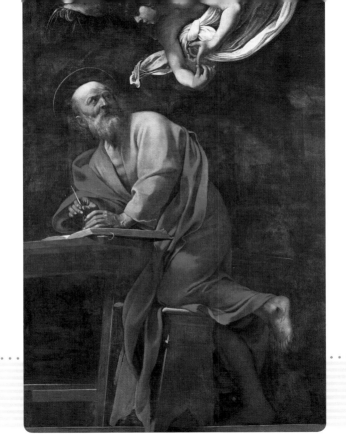

Crucifixion
of St Peter

n September 1600 Caravaggio had an important commission from Tiberio Cerasi, treasurer of Pope Clement VIII, for two paintings to place in the chapel he had purchased in the church of Santa Maria del Popolo. They were: "Crucifixion of St Peter" and "Conversion of St Paul". Both the canvases, in their first versions, were rejected by the rectors of the Hospital of the Consolazione. The following versions were accepted and displayed in the present setting.

Historically Peter and Paul represent the two pillars of the Church. In the "Crucifixion", Caravaggio refuses any detail of the setting and dwells only upon the characters, the saint and the three executioners. The poetic of the horrid used by Caravaggio in his scenes of martyrdom or, more generally, in representing death, is given up in this work in favour of a new conception of death, as a sort of "job". The clear tension, the physical effort of the executioners and St Paul surrendering as if following his executioners, characterize the atmosphere of the painting – here the tragedy gives place to the tension and dismay of pain.

▶

BIOGRAPHY

He had to stop at Porto Ercole, a Spanish possession on the border of the Papal State. Soon Caravaggio was arrested for a case of mistaken identity. On his release, he discovered that the felucca had already sailed. Baglione describes those last hours during which "he could not find the felucca and furiously he walked along that shore under the heat to see whether he could see at sea the vessel with his belongings".

St Peter's face, represented from a realistic point of view, is absolutely extraordinary: a poor old man suffering an absurd torture – the upside down crucifixion – as he himself had asked for his acknowledged inferiority to Jesus. As always in Caravaggio, the darkness around the characters is a means to point out the sharply illuminated figures, more than being a symbolic expression. ■

CRUCIFIXION OF ST PETER
1600/01 – Rome, Santa Maria del Popolo, detail

On that shore Caravaggio fell ill with malaria. He died on 18th July 1610. For a terrible twist of fate the papal clemency had been granted, and his admission to Rome allowed.

BIOGRAPHY

Conversion
of St Paul

*1600/01 – Rome,
Santa Maria del Popolo*

The difference between this painting and the first version in the Odescalchi Collection is huge. The Odescalchi version is dramatic, excited, full of tension, while this representation of the falling of Saul on the way to Damascus is the expression of a calm and almost ecstatic acceptance. The open-wide arms of the saint – which seem to embrace the divine light in a breathtaking and alive charm – are the lines of force of this "claustrophobic" representation. Christ and the angel of the first version are here only one intuition, absolutely invisible, represented by the hot gleam springing from the top right angle, as well as the figure of the horse – before scared and frightened – and here made according to a striking and immediate realism. ■

"No baroque forms can be found in Caravaggio. For his depth and clearness he goes back more to the 1400 artists than to his contemporaries. He has an epic depth in himself, a humanistic apostolic will, very far from the baroque behaviour: his inner formation represents his historical solitude in the Baroque and beyond."
C. L. Ragghianti

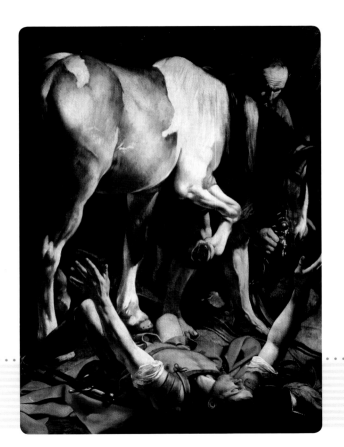

The Entombment

1602/04 – Vatican, Pinacoteca Vaticana

The "Entombment" in the Pinacoteca Vaticana was commissioned for the Vittrice Chapel in Santa Maria in Vallicella. The canvas is perhaps the most studied and admired of all Caravaggio's production – as a matter of fact there is a great number of copies and studies by artists such as Rubens, Géricault and Cézanne. The composition represents the right moment of the entombment of Christ. Caravaggio's interpretation is similar to the two canvases in Santa Maria del Popolo. Tragedy and piety are mitigated by the representation of tension, exemplified in the two figures holding the body of dead Christ. It is uncommon to find in a Caravaggesque work the execratory gesture made by Maria Cleofe: wide open arms. On the contrary, the livid complexion of Christ, which enlightens the scene as in a flash of light, is typical Caravaggesque. The work may have several symbolic interpretations. We seem to feel the real weight of Christ's body in the right moment in which it is entombed – the point of view of the observer is set inside the sepulchre. The material and the moral weight – that is the human pain – become blurred. ■

CRITICAL NOTES

"It is not the lack of each defect, but the presence of high qualities which make up a character or even a genius. Such men with their indomitable passion cannot resign themselves to the impeccable wisdom of mediocrity. Among them, Caravaggio..."
V. Schoelcher

Madonna
dei Palafrenieri

The work derives its name from the Confraternity of the Palafrenieri in the Vatican Palaces, which commissioned it for St Peter's chapel. According to the committers, the canvas had to be dedicated to St Anne. Really she was given less importance than the figures of the Madonna and her child crushing the serpent, who have been privileged. After few days, the canvas was removed because of theological reasons and its lack of "decorum". This work has deep symbolic contents; a Bull by Pius V clearly stated whose foot – Madonna's or Jesus' – had crushed the serpent, as Caravaggio represented the two feet one over the other. The "Madonna dei Palafrenieri" is characterized by a wise tonal and building balance. ■

The death
of the Virgin

1605/07
Paris, Louvre

The "Death of the Virgin" is a work of outstanding complexity and it was one of the most criticized paintings by Caravaggio.

The picture was commissioned for the Carmelite Church of Santa Maria della Scala in Trastevere, but the painting was not appreciated for its strong realism. The Virgin is portrayed with swollen womb and feet; an uncertain tradition says that the Madonna was modelled on a Roman prostitute, who was drowned in the Tiber. Highly appreciated by Rubens – who urged the Duke of Mantua Vincenzo Gonzaga to purchase it – for its baroque chromatic taste, the painting has in itself a dark sense of death and a charm for its human and religious intensity, infused in the person who looks at it. ■

Beheading of
Saint John the Baptist

1608 – Valletta, St. John Museum

The "Beheading of Saint John the Baptist" is the most important work made by Caravaggio in Malta. The canvas was commissioned by the Grand Master of the Order of Malta, Alof de Wignacourt, already portrayed in a picture today preserved in the Louvre. Many critics consider it Caravaggio's masterpiece and one of the most important works in Western painting. The scene develops in front of a prison building. Two figures at the window of which witness the scene. A classical style balance holds the structure of the composition. Worth noting is the detail of the trickle of blood from the neck of the Baptist which – spreading on the ground – forms the autograph signature of the artist. A seal in blood, highly symbolic and absolutely new in the history of art. ■

St John
the Baptist

*1609 – Rome,
Borghese Gallery*

The adolescent Baptist, "a handsome Roman young man, fond of pleasant idleness, so clever as to devote himself to contemplation" (Venturi, 1909), relaxed and weak-limped, is so different from the same subject portrayed in the canvas in the Capitoline Museums, more vigorous and alive, and in that kept in the Corsini Gallery, which has more psychological investigation. In the canvas, all centred in the figure of the saint, there is a strong red drapery, which recalls the pose of the Baptist himself and it is, at the same time, its

chromatic counterpoint. On the background there is a ram, symbol of luxury for some people, and branches of vegetation of high naturalistic and analytic carefulness, in contrast with late Caravaggio's executive impatience during the Neapolitan period. ■

David with the
head of Goliath

1609/10 – Rome,
Borghese Gallery

Painted for Cardinal Scipione Borghese between 1609 and 1610 during Caravaggio's second stay in Naples. Caravaggio portrayed himself in the head of Goliath and sent the work to the court of the Pope in Rome to receive the pardon in the hope to come back to Rome. Beyond its peculiar artistic virtues, the picture lays itself open to an historic analysis with stratified psychological and moral interpretations. The self-portrait is a sort of admission of guilt. In the image of David, Caravaggio seems to indulge on the moment in which piety imposes itself

on triumphant virtue: "I will strike you down, and cut off your head; and I will give the dead bodies of the host of the Philistines to the birds of the air and to the wild beasts; that all the earth may know that there is a God in Israel" (Samuel, 17, 46). ■

· ·

© **2004** roma editrice

roma editrice is a mark by
ATS Italia Editrice S.r.l.
Via di Brava 41/43 – 00163 Rome – Italy

Photo:
ATS Italia Editrice S.r.l. Archive
Scala Photographic Archive
PhotoService Electa
Vatican Museum Photographic Archive

The images of the Scala Photographic
Archive and PhotoService Electa which
reproduce the cultural heritage belonging
to the Italian State are published thanks
to the Ministry of National Heritage and
Culture

Text: Taken from: "Caravaggio"
by Andrea Pomella

Graphic project, paging and cover:
ATS Italia Editrice

Translation: Tiziana Vallocchia

Chromatic scanning and corrections:
ATS Italia Editrice (Ilaria Ratti)

Printing:
Papergraf s.p.a. – Piazzola sul Brenta (PD)

The editor is at disposal of all those who lay
claims to unfound iconographic sources

www.atsitalia.it

· ·

ISBN 88-7571-082-1